KU-794-861

SUCCESS
IS A FAILURE
EXPERIENCE

SUCCESS
IS A FAILURE
EXPERIENCE

*Male Liberation and the
American Myth of Success*

William L. Malcomson

ABINGDON PRESS
Nashville, Tennessee

SUCCESS IS A FAILURE EXPERIENCE

Copyright © 1976 by Abingdon Press

Library of Congress Cataloging in Publication Data

MALCOMSON, WILLIAM L. Success is a failure experience.
1. Success. 2. Men. I. Title.
BJ1611.M312   158′.1   75-33055

ISBN 0-687-40564-5

Scripture quotations noted TEV are from the Today's English
Version of the New Testament. Copyright © American Bible Society
1966.

MANUFACTURED BY THE PARTHENON PRESS AT
NASHVILLE, TENNESSEE, UNITED STATES OF AMERICA

Dedication

to Laurie, Christi, Scott, and John, who allow
me to be me and still be loved.

and to Karl, who named the demon.

Contents

PART I

The Bondage of the American Male
to the Myth of Success

Middle-aged men like me are hooked on the myth of success. We are enslaved, bound, trapped, by this myth. I have been programmed to succeed or give up the whole thing. Failure is not acceptable, not permitted—if you want to be a man. And this is what we who are products of the thirties and forties want to be—men. Not persons, *men*.

The myth of success, American version, is, to put it in its simplest form, that if you work hard enough, you will "make it." You will succeed in what you do, if you care enough about succeeding. Think positively about the possibility of your success, and you will be a success. Being a success means having a good job that provides security for your wife and children. It means doing what you want to do and making good at it. It means doing well in your job, in your home life, in bed, and in the eyes of other men and women, and in God's eyes.

This is our trap. For when you experience success, and I have experienced it—fully, happily, and with a great deal of excitement—you find out that it is a failure experience, it is binding, it is enslaving. Not necessarily in the short run. Not for years, sometimes. But then it comes, slowly, creeping up on you when you are alone or at night or in some airplane flying to another conference. You have opened the door of success, and you are not meeting yourself, you are looking at someone else. This is the failure experience—that has haunted me through the years since I heard Ross Snyder of Chicago Theological Seminary say, "Look at yourself and ask if someone else is living your life." That is the problem with success. Someone else is living your life. Another standard, another image, is defining your life. It is the male image—the image of masculine success. You are living that image; you are not living *you.* This is the bondage. Freedom comes only when *you* begin living your life.

What I propose to do in Part I of this book is to spell out, through a series of evocative, rather than descriptive, essays, how I feel about the situation of middle-aged men in this society, how we get defined vocationally, in the family, and religiously. In many of these essays I also touch on a few possibilities for hope, suggesting some themes which I develop in Part II.

There is a reason why I chose the categories of job, family, and religion in Part I. Men in our society are producers and are expected to define themselves as producers. The main arena for production is the job. Secondly, the male is expected to be a fine husband and father. The home is to be the cradle of success. In the third area, religion, I speak very autobiographically, being a deeply religious person. And I realize that I am speaking primarily to religious people. It seems to me that not enough has been said about the success cult in American religious life.

What I am doing is describing our bondage. If the chains fit, break them.

Success on the Job

The American male is a producer. The place where he does the major part of his producing is the world of work—on the job. Here is where the myth holds full sway. Therefore, I begin these essays on the myth of success, and man's bondage to it, with some thoughts about work.

These essays do not develop a thesis. They are more in the way of thrusts and parries. One may not "hit" you, but another will. Give them a try. I think you will recognize yourself before very long.

Justifying Our Existence

A: I feel free!

B: What do you mean, free?

A: Free to be, just to be. Free as the wind.

B: That's fine for you, but I don't feel that way at all.

A: Why not?

B: Well, I have certain obligations, things I have to do. I can't "cop out."

A: You can be who you are, can't you?

B: Not all the time. No, indeed. I am not even sure who I am all the time. I can't do what I want all the time.

A: What's tying you down?

B: Oh, you know—my job, my family, my whole style of living.

A: Just be who you are. Like me—free!

B: I am free, in a way. But I also have responsibilities. Like making a living, feeding the family. That sort of thing.

A: Oh, sure, but making a living isn't all that hard. You have a good job. Be free.

B: I would like to hold on to that good job. And, besides, it isn't only a matter of making a living. I like my job, for the most part. At least basically.

A: Can you be free in your job?

B: Free? Certainly. But I have responsibilities. And it isn't only me by myself in my job. I relate to other people, and I feel responsible to and for them to a degree.

A: You're really getting hemmed in.

B: I don't actually feel so hemmed in. I feel needed. My job is needed. Those who hired me need me. The people with whom I work need me. I am important where I am.

A: But are you free?

B: I guess I am as free as I can be. Freedom to me doesn't mean that I can do anything I want to do or "be who I am" all the time. I have to accommodate and be who I am needed to be at the time or by a particular person. And, in a way, that is who I am too.

A: But all those obligations. Are you saying that that is freedom?

B: Not entirely, but it is being useful.

A: You know what you are trying to do, don't you? You are trying to justify your existence by being of use.

Your existence doesn't need justifying. It is enough
to be and to be you.

B: I don't buy that. I have to be me, and I have to be
useful, too. I continually have to prove to others and
myself that I am of use.

A: Then you aren't free.

B: Being free isn't all that great, then. But being a
useful person, a person who is accomplishing something, being significant—that is important to me.

In spite of all that Christianity and a number of other
religious faiths say about the acceptance of the person
by God, and about forgiveness, most of us still feel the
necessity of justifying our existence—or, as we might
put it, "proving ourselves." We do not really believe
that we can just "*be*" and that that is all that is needed.
Possibly this is as it should be. I doubt if much would be
accomplished in the world if we didn't spend some time
trying to justify our existence.

In America the male justifies his existence by
production. He produces a family, a home, and he
produces work on the job. He produces an image—
status, position in the community, whatever you may
like to call it. He is a producer.

For me, the problem arises when a man sees himself
as only a producer and nothing else. Or when he has
bought the myth that only he is the producer, and his
wife cannot be, or other women cannot be.

Do I have to divide my day between producing and
being? On the job: producing. At home: being.

It isn't that neat, is it? When I am on the job, I am

trying to be free and open and relaxed with the people I work with. When I am home, I am often accomplishing something—in the garden, in the house, in interaction with the wife and kids. The trick is not to think of myself as always, every moment of the day, having to produce, to prove myself, to accomplish something. If I did that, I would never relax, never wind down, never renew my strength. Maybe it takes an ulcer to find that out—to find out that being a human being in our society means proving yourself, and not proving yourself.

Women can produce, too.

Sure, they can produce babies. And a pleasant home.

No, I mean producing in the business world, in the services sector, in professional life. Is it unfeminine to produce? Or do we who are men think that women do this sort of thing (work) because they aren't happy at home or they want to imitate men or they don't know their place? I would imagine that they want to produce because they are human. *Persons* are producers— female persons, male persons. Don't people get bored sitting around just "being"? I would say that each of us has a production need and a being need. The balance varies with each person. But this has little (or nothing?) to do with being a man or a woman.

Measuring Up

A: I'm not sure if I am a success—if I measure up or not.

B: Do you think that there is some kind of a standard for judging?

A: Of course. You have to measure up to some standard. People expect you to accomplish certain things or you aren't a success.

B: Then the standard is other people's expectations?

A: Sure. Everybody has some idea of what makes up success. In my field we have standards of measurement. Then people who are above you decide whether or not you measure up to these standards.

B: That sounds sort of dehumanizing.

A: If you want to be a success, you can't just do your own thing, you know.

B: I don't mean doing your own thing. But what I mean is that if you always have to measure up to some external standard, then what good is it to be *you?* I would think that a lot of people could measure up to such standards. You aren't unique.

A: I never said I was unique. No one is indispensable. Not even the top executive.

B: But I think that you *are* really unique. I am unique. And in a way, I am indispensable. There is no one else who is me, and there never will be again. I am the only me there is.

A: O.K. That's true in your relationship with your family and your friends and so on, but the job is a different thing.

B: But it is on the job that I make most of my contribution. I want my contribution to be unique.

A: But you can't just do your own thing.

B: If it isn't at least partly my own unique thing, then I am only a cog in a machine, a card with a number on it.

17

A: You will never be a success if you want to go off and do only what you want to do.

B: I don't want to go off on my own. I want to work in an organization. But I want to be recognized for my uniqueness, for what I—me—I have to contribute.

A: Don't count on an employer buying that. Most of them know what they want. And if you don't fit their image, you are *out*, charlie!

A Suggestion

Is it too far out in left field to say that I want to measure up to my own standard and not be captured by the standards of others? I want to be my own judge. Whether that is too far out or not, that is what I want.

I have the feeling that I can even be paid to be me. Sure, I have to have some marketable skills. And I am paid to use these skills. But I can use them in my own unique manner, and I can prove to those who hired me that there is a difference between me using these skills and someone else using them. I not only set my own standard, I convince others that my standard which I set for me is a valid standard, even in their eyes.

Now this doesn't mean that I can do anything I want to do, and ignore other people. I have to work with people and respect them and gain their respect. But having my own way all the time is not being me either. Being isolated and doing my own thing by myself is not me. I guess that what I mean is I do not want to be judged solely by a standard which could work for anyone. I don't want to be "electrician," "clerk," "teacher," or whatever—I WANT TO BE MY NAME.

The title is somewhat descriptive, but only somewhat; it does not define who I am.

Phrases Overheard

A: What shall we do for the first meeting of this committee?
B: Well, Mr. Chairman, what did last year's committee do?

A: What do you think of Sam's work?
B: He doesn't turn out the amount of stuff that Jack did.

He is a nice enough guy, but he isn't my idea of what a minister should be.

A: He really cannot handle responsibility.
B: What has he failed at recently?
A: It isn't that so much. You meet him once and you'll see what I mean.

A: He doesn't fit what I have in mind.
B: Well, you certainly wouldn't want to hire someone you can't work with.

"This person is not your basic 'Savior' type. Too young and inexperienced. For one thing, he didn't get into the business until he was thirty. Then he got himself into trouble pretty quickly. I mean, he really went off the deep end. One problem was that he didn't seem to have a clear idea of his goal. Sometimes he would heal a lot of people, and other times he would not heal at all. He couldn't seem to stay in one place very long. Took up with a group that was not representative of the best in our culture. Said a lot of things that made very little sense. To give an example, he spoke in parables rather than straight out. Seldom defined his terms. Never fit in at all, even though he seemed to want to make headway with those in power. Didn't look very promising from the start, and when he was executed I said, 'Good riddance.' No, he never measured up to my idea of a Savior.

"Now, you take the Pharisees—there were some promising fellows in that group."

When All Else Fails—Work

One of the most acceptable ways for a man to deal with his frustrations is to work, to pour himself into his job. Work is great therapy, so the myth goes.

Things aren't going too well at home, the kids and I are getting farther and farther apart, so I put myself more fully into my work. If I keep busy I will forget. And, besides, work by its very nature accomplishes something (and I am accomplishing nothing at home).

They keep asking me to do more and more things in the church, in the community, and I don't want to. So I will work longer hours at the office ("Love to do it, but the work is piling up, you know—maybe next time"), attend more meetings, go to more conferences ("Have to be out of town a lot this month, otherwise I would sure love to"). Everyone understands. "Old Bill has been working awfully hard lately."

The wife keeps saying, "Let's take some time off, honey, and go up to the lake for the weekend." But I am afraid that if I do, I will have to deal with the long-smoldering hostility between us, and I don't have the strength for that. So I say, "I'd love to, sweetie, but the boss is really pouring it on this month."

One of the great things about work is that it makes you feel needed.

A: You know, Jack, we need a man like you to tackle the advertising for that new line. I have wracked my brain trying to think of someone, but I can't think of anyone who can match your capability.

B: I appreciate that, and I think I can work it in. Things are a little slower this month ["the boss is really pouring it on this month"]. I would like to see what I could do with it. It would be a challenge.

A: I like you, Jack. You have a spirit of adventure.

Now who gets this kind of affirmation at home?

Another good thing about work is that it keeps you busy. In fact, it has a narcotic effect. You take it and you keep busy and you forget all your worries. Instead of taking a pill, you go to the office. ("Old Fred really burns the midnight oil. He's going to be head of this company someday.") You pack up your cares and woes in a briefcase and head for work. And it is acceptable. You are busy, you are affirmed, you are contributing to the good of the society.

Work is so moral. Who can knock it? "If we could all

give ourselves to our work as Pete does, there would be a lot less problems here. He is a dedicated man." To lose yourself in the service of the firm, others, society, God, —, —. Nothing more noble than that. It is self-sacrificing, anti-egotistical—pouring out your life as a ransom for many (Matt. 26:28). There is a messianic aspect in hard work.

Does work deal with your frustrations? Do you pill yourself to sleep so that you won't lie awake thinking about your problems that have been submerged in a sea of work all day? Does work bridge the gap between you and your wife, does it fill in the cracks in the broken relationship with your kids?

I have opened all the doors but one.
Tasted all the wines but one.
Slept in all the beds but one.
And that one haunts me. I want to turn the knob, but I am afraid.
Afraid of the mirror behind it, the tears that will greet me, the seeing no longer through a glass, darkly, but now being seen—face to Face.
All the doors but one—the door to me.
All the wines but one—the wine of my life.
All the beds but one—the one I shall lie in forever.

Castration or Seduction

I would argue that a man in our society can be either castrated or seduced. Of the two, he is probably most afraid of castration.

A: I gave in. I wanted so much to be liked that I went along with what he said even though I did not believe a word of it.

B: You lied?

A: No, I didn't lie, but I didn't push for the truth.

B: Could you have pushed for the truth?

A: Sure, if I had taken the risk of making him my enemy. I wasn't strong enough to take the risk. I didn't stand up to him like a man. What he was saying was so ridiculous. But I sat there and let him say it, not wanting to antagonize him or have him dislike me.

B: You feel kind of castrated—right?

A: Right. I feel like I've let my manhood be taken from me. I didn't stand up. I didn't fight him or even try to push my way in.

A: She laid me out. Really gave it to me.

B: What did you do?

A: I said something she didn't like and she let me know it.

B: What did you do then?

A: I took it. Looked sort of sheepish and thanked her for being honest with me.

B: You didn't fight back?

A: It wouldn't have done any good.

B: She's a real tiger, huh?

A: Claws that big—you know?

A: I knew that this would be it. I worked for it for years, and finally my time had come. I knew this would be the day.

B: What happened?

A: The other guy got the position. Can you imagine that?

B: He didn't deserve it?

A: Hell, no. He was new, green, unproven. Oh, he was impressive. Had a lot of degrees. And he had some luck in bringing off a couple of recent projects. But I was the obvious choice.

B: Did you say anything to the boss?

A: What good would it do? He's got the power.

B: Just cut you off at the pockets.

A: All that work, for all those years, down the drain.

To be a man is to stand up for what you are, for what you deserve, for your rights. To refuse to do so, to let another person push you around, is to be castrated. It is to have your masculinity cut off. For a man, this is the worst thing that can happen. If you are a man and you are not acting like a man, then you are nothing. If you have lost your masculinity, you are neither male nor female. You are sexless and powerless. Most men in our society believe that most of us males are castrated. There are very few real "studs" around anymore.

What about seduction?

A: Let's go and tell him off. If a couple of us get together and do it, nothing and no one can stop us.

B: Right! We can get some power going then. We can push right in there and really let him have it.

A: Are you with me?

B: You better believe it, buddy. I've wanted to get him for years.

A: When you work with women, you have to tease them along.

B: How do you mean?

A: Play up to them. Act the he-man. Protect them, make them think you are taking care of them.

B: Like being a lover, so to speak.

A: Most of their husbands are lousy lovers, anyway. You can usually count on that. So you love the women, or act as if you do. In a way, you are a safe image of what they really want a man to be.

B: And this works with the women you work with?

A: Yeah. They think I'm great. I'm big stuff. I think they secretly wish I would go to bed with them. But I am not going to be seduced into that. Then, you see, I would lose power over them. The trick is to tease, but not produce.

A: We need a person of your caliber in this position. It is a new venture for us, and we want someone with your kind of imagination.

B: I'm always willing to try something new and creative.

A: Good. I like conviction and self-confidence.

B: I always take pride in my work. I want to do something that is done right, and that I can be proud of.

A: I like a man like that. Makes us all feel good.

B: I'll do the best I can. You will never be sorry you hired me.

A: I'm sure of that. You younger men are the real future of this company.

The subtle thing about coming out on top is that usually you have been seduced into it. What appears to be initiative and strength is often a matter of being bought at an attractive price. A friend calls you to the colors, to exercise your hate (a fine masculine trait), and you are all for it. But you are being seduced. You tease the women, acting the strong man, the lover. But you are being seduced into the *Playboy* image. And you are seducing yourself. The boss tells you how great you are and you believe it. It doesn't look like seduction, because it feels so good, but he is seducing you.

The odd thing about seduction in our society is that it is castrating. The odd thing about castration is that it is taken so seriously, as if the whole world were going down the tubes. When a man's masculinity is cut off, he thinks he is no longer a human being.

Whatever happened to being yourself?

Who said I couldn't give in? Who said I have to fight back? Who said I can't be hurt by another person? Who said I have to hate in order to be a man? Who said I have to act like a "stud"?

The idea is to be neither castrated nor seduced, or, if you are, to know it and accept it and say, "Yes, that's me all right." The idea is to know what you are doing and what is being done to you. To know who you are, even when being castrated or seduced. Who you are can rise above both of these.

What actually castrates is the power of an image

which is not who I am. What actually seduces is the image of what I wish I were but am not. The true lie is to tell myself that I am not what I should be, or to say I am something I am not.

Don't be cut off and don't be sucked in—unless you are being true to yourself. And if that is the case, then it won't seem like castration or seduction anyway.

Climbing to the Top

The game of success involves either doing a job better than other people do it or convincing someone over you that you can do a better job, or both. If I had to choose between convincing and doing, I would opt for doing. Doing is the most powerful and lasting way of convincing.

However you slice it, when you do a better job than someone else and this moves you closer to the top, you are climbing over other people. Doing a better job than another person is competing with him and beating him. What you are actually doing is profiting from his inadequacy.

The game:

I think I can do a better job than Joe.

I do a better job than Joe.

The boss knows that it is a better job.

I move higher than Joe.

You could call this becoming indispensable. I can do the job so well that it looks as if no one else could do it. So I do it. I am relied upon to do it. Every time someone wants it done, I do it. I am designated as the only one who can do it. If you create a job, this works even better. You thought up the job and you put it into operation. It is your "thing" and it won't go without you.

Don't you really think that all this stuff about "I will be a success when I work myself out of a job" is a lot of false piety? I am a success if I work myself into a job, particularly if it is one that no one else can do. Or, rather, no one else thinks he can do it—or, more importantly, the boss thinks that no one else can do it.

Have you discovered that in order to move up, you have to develop a rather hardened attitude toward other employees? If you don't it can hurt to move up. Or you might get involved in the problems of those who are stepped on (this is particularly rough if you are the one who is doing the stepping).

Let us now turn to *acceptable* ways of climbing over other people—acceptable in our society, that is.

1. "What we need around here is more dynamic leadership."

Who can disagree with that? What you mean, of course, is that the present leaders are not cutting the mustard. You convince the boss that more dynamic leadership is needed, and that you are a dynamic leader—therefore, you are needed. If he agrees with your definition of "dynamic" (or "creative," "farsight-ed," etc.), you are in. You have begun, you see, by making a judgment on the present employees, but you have put it in impersonal terms. This is quite accept-able. You forge ahead.

2. "We are doing a good job, but we could do better."

Obviously. Then the boss says, "How could we do a better job?" Here is where you come in. You define "a better job," and it turns out to include what you do best. Now this is also acceptable. You have used impersonal terms. What you really mean, of course, is that your fellow employees are inadequate.

3. "Why don't we establish priorities and concentrate on those?"

Who can argue against this? Establishing priorities always gets a hearing. When we do this, we find that out of ten items we are really concerned about five. We decide to concentrate on the five. This means, of course, that those who were engaged in the other five areas of work are out. It also means that you are farsighted, because you helped us to concentrate on essentials. The chances are that you have worked it so that one of the top priorities is a job that you do best. Again, this is impersonal and acceptable. It is a matter of priorities, not of people.

4. "We need some new blood around here."

Absolutely. If you happen to be under forty-five, you may look like new blood. But even if you are not, you might promise to recruit some new blood. Either way, you can climb up. It will mean firing some people, and hiring those who agree with you on what is meant by "new blood." "New blood" may sound a bit personal, but it is not. It is an impersonal term, even though it actually refers to climbing over some "old-blooded" people.

I would challenge you to name a situation where moving ahead does not require pushing someone else out of the way, or, at least, down the ladder. Not that you necessarily do it directly. But you have done it indirectly or have been the recipient of the benefits when someone else has done it. Success is always a commodity which is bought at a price. The cost is paid by you and by other people. Other people may pay by being pushed back or by staying in the same place. You pay by realizing that you have not only stepped *up* but stepped *on*. And this tends to make you a little harder, a little more impersonal, and, perhaps, a little more lonely.

Does this sound like a book by Machiavelli? O.K. But look at it this way for a moment: in our society, there are those who lead and those who follow, those who move ahead and those who stay where they are or move back. This is the way it is. I am not convinced that it is necessarily bad. I have more problems with religious people who act as if this is not the way it is, than with religious people who know that this is the way it is, who don't particularly enjoy it, but who have learned to live with it. We are human. We are not God. God can look out for everyone's welfare, but we cannot. God doesn't have to succeed, but many of us are "wired up" that way. He—God—knows that he is "O.K.," but you and I aren't too sure about ourselves.

What does all this look like from the side of the failure—the one who got pushed back or who stayed in the same slot? This is a human situation. It would be great if everyone were appreciated, but it just isn't so. Some are more appreciated than others. Not everyone is a success—and not everyone will be, no matter how hard they try. Why not face up to it? It is not always bad to get pushed back. Maybe you are a pushed-back person and you ought to face up to it. You pay a price. But the guy on top pays a price also—ulcers, high blood pressure, loneliness.

Is it possible that success is a failure experience? Well, any time you climb over another, you succeed but you also fail. A little of your humanity gets chopped off. Can failure be a success experience? Yes, for when you fail you may succeed in facing up to who you are. The whole thing is being who you are—right?

Success in the Home

The second major arena for the man is the home. Here he is again called upon to produce—to be the husband, father, provider, sexual performer. The essays in this group take a look at the various aspects of the world of the home. The last two deal with sex. They are frank and earthy. I decided to do one on homosexuality because I am becoming increasingly aware of the extent of this life-style and of its implications for those of us who are heterosexually inclined.

I caricature a bit here, but I do it for a purpose. A caricature can be a little off center, but it often enables us to see that the truth has qualities of the ludicrous. In laughing at the caricature, we laugh at ourselves. Don't we?

My Family Has the Best

If a father can't provide the best for his family, what good is he? That is the mark, isn't it?

"He takes care of his family."

"He has always been a good provider."

"Frank has done his best by his family, and that is all you can ask of a man."

The best: food, nice clothes, a fine home, a good education, a sense of security, plans for the future.

It isn't that we were taught only to give them *things*. A good environment was also important, and a sense of being cared for and cared about. A certain kind of psychological atmosphere, always positive, and one which spurred them on to greater achievements. It isn't rampant materialism—more a matter of rampant well-being.

Rest assured that it is "my" family. I feel responsible for the whole group. My job is to protect them from harm, keep them healthy, help them to move toward adulthood (am I speaking only of the kids?—oh, no, for the American male of my generation thinks of himself as training his wife as well, bringing her up to be a good wife and a mature person), and see that they are taken care of should anything happen to me. The home is the haven. The fence is up (if not literally, then psychologically), the gate is open only for those for whom we choose to open it, and we resent any intrusion of noise, destruction of property, or nosiness. If we could afford a moat, we would probably get one. For this is my home, my castle, my "private space."

You who are younger need to understand this protectiveness in order to understand the race to the suburbs, the attitudes toward busing and neighborhood schools, and the basic republicanism of my generation. We are protecting our chicks. This is our responsibility.

When you enter my home, you ask if you may come. Private property is not a matter of real estate, it is a matter of not violating my (and, by extension, "our") being. Many of my generation are against busing because we are afraid our kids will get hurt in that rough world out there. We are a rather paranoid group as a whole, because the world has moved so fast that we are afraid that everything is going to crumble ("future shock"). We want to make sure that we have built our own bombshelter and that we know who is going to occupy it.

All this assumes that as the father I know what is best. That is a big assumption. I know I don't know best, but I don't want them (the family) to know it, so I act as if I knew best. I make pronouncements on matters that really are beyond me.

"But why, Daddy?"

"Because I (or your mother and I) say so, that's why."

I arbitrate disputes when I haven't the foggiest notion what should be done. But my impulses are better than theirs because I am the father. My assumption is that my role gives me some kind of direct line to God the Father—automatically, it isn't something I necessarily think out. Wisdom is given with fatherhood, as grass is green and water is wet. You ask any father between the ages of thirty-five and fifty-five; he may deny it, but he believes it. Watch him with his wife and his kids. You'll see. He makes the decisions, establishes the rules, wields the power. (Unless he abdicates the power to his wife. Some of my peers do this. But we look down on them. Being "henpecked" is almost worse than being a homosexual.) The success of a man's fatherhood depends, not on the objective wisdom of his decisions, but on the positive response of the family to those decisions. If they follow his orders, they are a good family and he is a good dad. If not, "it's mutiny, and by God, I'll see you hanged for that, Mr. Christian!"

The weariness of this burden-bearing is sometimes too much. I don't want to provide, make decisions, or protect. Just let me get in the car, drive to a nice river, and fish for the rest of my life. Or ride the rails. Anything to get away. I am not God, don't want to be, and in no way am cut out for the job. Do you wonder why middle-aged men disappear? They can't take divinity any longer.

The castle is crumbling. To hell with the moat.

Like a Rock

A: The little woman has her problems, no question about that.

B: Your wife is sick?

A: No, not physically. She just has a lot to cope with.

B: Like what?

A: Oh, you know—the kids, the house, her activities.

B: She must keep busy all right.

A: I try to provide some security for her. Keep her happy.

B: How do you mean?

A: Well, I don't bring problems home from the office.

At home I am the strong husband who holds her in my arms and protects her.

B: I'll bet she likes that.

A: Calls me her "rock." She says she doesn't know what she would do if I weren't so strong.

B: I guess you better stay healthy.

A: Wish I were as secure as she thinks I am.

B: Come again?

A: Problems at work. My job may be phased out.

B: At your age?

A: Yeah, there's a good chance of it.

B: Have you told you wife?

A: Oh, no, she couldn't take it. She would fall apart. I'm her rock.

We men can be so alone. That is why so many rush to mistresses or psychiatrists or ministers or anyone who will listen. And some can't do that. They stay alone and try to bluff it through. Without the help of the wife—the "little woman," "baby." We have to be her security, her rock, her strength.

Do we?

Is it strong to hide your problems? Is it strong to refuse to share your deepest concerns with the one whom you say you love? ("God purposely chose . . . what the world considers weak in order to put powerful men to shame" [I Cor. 1:27 TEV].) Maybe she can't take it? How do you know? And if she can't take it, in the sense of standing there like a rock, does that mean she can't take it? Maybe crying with you is the best way. Or have you been afraid to test your relationship? Perhaps your love is built on a very weak foundation, and it could crumble so easily it scares you.

I have no doubt that many wives want security. But at the price of dishonesty? So many wives say that their husbands do not communicate with them. Maybe we underestimate our wives. Perhaps they can take more than we think they can. Or is it that we do not want to admit our need? Our need to be a rock, but also to be at times a crumbling wall that desperately needs support, shoring up, some new cement. Is it so awful to admit that to my wife?

A tall, straight tree stands in the forest. It is strong, secure, imposing. But without nourishment, it will die. Without the humus on the forest floor, without the water seeping into its roots, without the sun, without the bugs that eat the other bugs that could kill it, it will die. The strongest need nourishment to maintain their strength. The tree could not go it alone. It is part of an environment, an interdependent system. And so am I. And so are you. Rocks never cry: but men do—if not to their wives to their mistresses, if not to their mistresses to a "shrink," if not to a "shrink" to themselves, or, maybe, to their God. But you do cry, even if no sound escapes.

What have we done to ourselves, that we try to be rocks instead of men?

Be a Pal to Your Son

When I was growing up, I used to hear that a father was supposed to be a pal to his son. A kind of older

37

buddy. My dad never was, and sometimes I wondered a bit whether I was missing something. I thought of Dad as Dad—an older person who provided security, who could be trusted, and who had definite views on how I should act and made those views known. But he wasn't a pal.

Have you ever tried being a pal to your son? The other day I suggested, "Hey, maybe I could go with you on that fifty-mile hike that the Scouts are taking into the Sierras." First reaction: incredulity. Second reaction: "Sure, that would be fine, though you know that I couldn't spend much time with you, Dad." He wanted to be with his Scout buddies and do a lot of stuff that might not include me. So much for being a pal to your son.

But we want to be successful fathers to our sons—right? After all, daughters are fine, but sons are sort of us in miniature. We can communicate our masculinity to them and watch them grow up as spitting images of incredible us. We have an investment in them, a lot at stake personally, and this just isn't as true with daughters. So we feel guilty if we aren't performing with the son as a father should.

Dammit, I am thirty years older than he is, and I have my own life! Why should I spend a lot of time with him when I really enjoy doing my own thing? So what do I do? I do what I like doing and invite him to do it with me if he wants to. Sometimes he does and sometimes he doesn't. Is that being a pal? Not really, because I have the upper hand. I do more determining than he does. I have more power.

Now maybe you are one of those fathers who are afraid. What is the kid going to amount to?

"I'm afraid my son may do what I did at his age. I want to keep him from that. I made a lot of mistakes, and I don't want him to make the same mistakes I did. So I'd better stick with him and find some interests we have in common and pursue those with him, or God only knows how he might end up or who he might take up with."

In other words, you want to protect him. So you act like a pal, an older friend, in order to protect him and keep him from other kids who would be bad influences. Or you choose his friends for him and take them along on your "pally" activities. You learn to sail, and you take him sailing. You learn to play football and you play football with him. You learn to climb mountains, etc. But above all, don't let him make mistakes, don't let him get out of your reach, don't let him grow up.

You will never be a pal, and you will never protect your son. He needs pals his own age, and people who have no power over him, unlike you. For however hard you try to be on his level, you have power over him, fella, and don't you forget it. He knows it, and he can resent it if you play like it isn't there. And he will grow up in spite of you. If you protect him when he is young, he will be unprotected in a frightening way when he gets older. So he might as well learn how to protect himself now.

We could be such interesting people to our children if we weren't so hung up on useless images. Who knows, your son might enjoy you as you are: a middle-aged, reasonably likeable guy who has his problems but is "making it"—to a degree, depending on the day and whether you have a headache or not. Your son is going to be an adult someday. Maybe he ought to know that being an adult like you isn't so bad. In fact, he might even grow to enjoy it. Like you do?

Your Daughter Should Look Up to You

A: My daughter is my pride and joy.

B: Really something, eh?

A: She looks up to me as if I were a god.

B: Is that good?

A: Why, sure. Don't you think it does my old ego a lot of good?

B: I suppose so.

A: I can do no wrong in her eyes.

B: My daughter isn't like that.

A: No?

B: No, she treats me as one of the family. Necessary to have around, but no god.

A: Well, my daughter worships me.

B: Boy, I don't know if I would want to be "under the gun" that much.

A: I love it, just love it. And I always give her what she wants. A soft touch—that's me.

That daughter is no dummy. She knows that her middle-aged father wants to be catered to and treated like a god. So she does it and she gets her way. We men want our daughters to look up to us whether or not our wives do (and particularly if they don't). We are sort of substitute husbands until they get husbands of their own. Then they will look up to their husbands, assuming that the boy is as great a guy as I am—right? We want to give the daughter a good male image, so that she won't go wrong when the time comes for selecting a husband. (You didn't know that women select their husbands? That is one of my generation's myths: the woman does the selecting and makes the man think he did it. It is a little game we play which we have always thought was harmless.)

Of course, if you are a god to your daughter you can't admit to any failure. Gods don't fail. And you can't get angry with her. It is all right to get angry at sons, because we expect more of them, and it teaches them forcefulness, but that won't wash with daughters. We tease them and "get in our licks" that way. And daughters know that we aren't too serious. They can get away with it again, because we can't come down from our pedestal.

I think it was James Baldwin who said that blacks know whites better than whites know themselves. It is the same with daughters. They know their dad better than he knows himself. They know how to manipulate him and feed his ego and when to give him favors and when to withdraw them.

But I wonder—couldn't my daughter handle me as I am? Maybe she would like me better as a human being, even though she would have to sacrifice some manipulation and wouldn't get her way with me as much. I am really not such a bad person when I am not playing like a god. In fact, I am rather endearing with my faults and foibles and all. These silly father-daughter games can be exhausting.

Men as Sexual Performers

It is amazing how free we are in many areas of our lives, and yet how rigid in terms of sexual expectations. It is a cardinal tenet of the myth of success that the male is to be a sexual performer in a very tightly prescribed way.

The male is the aggressor in sexual intercourse. Every time the male engages in intercourse, he is to have an orgasm. The female is to fully enjoy the experience of intercourse every time, or the male has failed. The male who engages in intercourse with great frequency is more masculine than the one who does not. Top performance is mutual orgasm, as often as possible. The male who really performs in bed is the healthy male. The male who does not perform according to the standard is sick, a failure, less than a man.

A man cannot fail in sex (which, in our society, always means intercourse between a man and a woman) and still be a man. So, of course, no man ever admits that he is a failure. The myth is kept alive through lying. When men get together, they talk in open or veiled ways about their sexual conquests—their performances. If you are a man, you could probably count on the fingers of half a hand how many times you have heard a fellow male admit to failure in the area of sex (unless you are a psychiatrist, and, if you are, that is cheating). The myth is perpetuated because it is understood that no one admits failure. In fact, I would contend that this is the only area in all of life where it is understood that you don't admit failure. A man in our society can admit that he is not a great parent, not too good a family man, even that he is not too outstanding in his job, but to admit that he has failed sexually is verbal suicide.

What we actually have in this country is a tremendous number of men who have failed at sex but are keeping it to themselves. The guilt that is carried on their shoulders is enough to hold up Manhattan Island for a millenium.

Would you believe that there are men, heterosexual men, living in this nation, who have never experienced mutual orgasm with a woman? And would you further believe that these men, though they feel guilty, or, at least, inadequate, are basically "making it" in society? How about this one: there are men who only have an orgasm once in a while, who never really satisfy their wives in the traditional sense, who are basically very happily married persons. Do you believe that? I do. How's that for your myth?

Man: Honey, how is it that I can love you and you love me and our sex life stinks?

Woman: I give up, how is it?

M: I don't know. Does it bother you?

W: Not really.

M: But I'm not doing what a man is supposed to be doing. I am not performing on schedule.

W: I think you're fine.

M: But I don't fit the image!

W: Thank God. I don't know if I could handle it if you did.

M: Maybe we're weird, abnormal, or something.

W: Oh, I don't know. A lot of wives I know don't think their sex lives are so fantastic.

M: Do you suppose that the guys who write the sex manuals are lying?

W: Probably they are dreaming.

Remember when you were a teen-ager? You figured that all your friends were having it great, and you were miserable. Then when you got older you discovered that most of them were miserable during their teen years too. We can hide a lot from each other, can't we?

Perhaps there ought to be a club called "A Club for Failures at Sex Who Have Great Marriages." My feeling is that the majority of American males who are happily married would join if they could remain anonymous.

One time I was talking with a man who was on the verge of a divorce. I asked him in the course of the conversation how he and his wife were doing sexually. He answered, "Great! No problem there." I knew that his wife had been having an affair with another man for some months prior to this time. But she and her husband had a great sex life. What he meant was that they could both perform during intercourse. A lousy marriage, but great sex. An American myth?

It is human to fail. Having an orgasm does not make you a man. Or a woman. What is inhuman is to live a

44

myth, to fear admitting that you don't fit the prevailing image. You and I are so hung up on images, we often have very little time to be human beings.

Sex, I would maintain, is taken much too seriously in our culture. What would happen if all lovers decided to engage in sexual abstinence for six months? I know a lot of women who would be a good deal happier, and a number of men who would shed a considerable amount of guilt. Not a bad idea. Do you think we could get a political candidate to run on that platform? Don't put money on it.

Homosexuality Is Nausea

One thing the real man would never be is "gay." I mean NEVER. Even the slightest inkling that you were tending that way would be occasion for revulsion. Male jokes fall into two main categories: the largest is jokes about treating women as objects for sexual conquest; the second largest is jokes about "fairies." But though "gays" are made fun of, the real reaction of the successful man is nausea.

A: They found out Jack was a fruitcake.
B: No! Good Lord!
A: Yeah, he hadn't been to bed with his wife for months.
B: She knew it?
A: Knew it, but didn't want it to get out.
B: I feel sorry for her. What an awful thing to live with.
A: Jack was shacking up with some artist over in Sausalito. On weekends.

B: Playing with each other. Makes you want to throw up.

A: If that's the way he wants to live his life.

B: If that's a life.

You catch yourself reacting to a known "gay" by wondering if he is flirting with you. Which is an interesting reaction, because it suggests that you, a full-blooded masculine man, could be attractive to another man. And when you think about it, you begin to gag. But there it is.

I can remember when men in our society didn't touch each other except to shake hands. My father and I always kiss each other when we first see each other or when we are taking leave of each other, but even with us there is very little touching during the general course of the day's activities. Men learned to be physically repelled when touched by a man. And now all sorts of artful games have to be played in "sensitivity groups" in order to get any genuinely felt touching. To touch a man is to act like a "queer," to show tenderness which is applicable only in male-female relationships. Except, of course, in contact sports. Then it is fine. Then you are fighting each other, and competitiveness is good and very manly. Two wrestlers can spend virtually the whole time mauling each other, but that is fine compared to a man putting his arm around a male friend.

Is affection out for the man who wants to succeed? Yes, except toward women. Partly, I would imagine, because affection suggests a need. If I am affectionate toward you, I need you. But to need another man is not manly. Men can need each other in team efforts which move toward goals, but they are not to need each other in terms of warmth and closeness, or like that. Women are for that. The image is of the tall man, rising above it all, needing no one but himself and bristling with achievement.

Is the fear of homosexuality related to a fear of being found out as one who needs affection, affirmation, and intimacy, even from those of your own sex? The nausea is a fear reaction. It is too much to take, isn't it, to realize that even you might be a little strange? Then the myth would be shot, wouldn't it? For a myth cannot allow for degrees, gradations, movement along a spectrum.

Success in Religion

Not all of us are religious; but for those of us who are, the success myth has played a major role in that aspect of our lives. A lot has been written about American religion and the differences between the Christian gospel and the faith of Americans. I am not interested in rehashing that material. My job is to be more personal, and to reflect what I have heard and what I have felt—particularly as it relates to the bondage of the American male to religious success. We groan under a yoke that must be named.

There is a certain amount of sarcasm in this group of essays, and a larger dose of personal purgation. I know whereof I speak, having been an active churchman and confessing Christian since before I knew what either of these phrases meant. My quarrel with the religion of my generation is a lovers' quarrel.

They Must Be Doing Something Right

"Jack and I were over at the community church the other day. Since that church is becoming so well known, we wanted to see for ourselves what is happening. They had three morning services, and the place was packed at each service And in the evening the service was led by the young people. Why, there must have been five hundred kids there. The church is building more facilities—a day care center, a senior citizens' high-rise, and a new gym. It's the biggest thing going in the city. They must be doing something right."

According to the myth of success, if something is successful it must be right. More production means more work, a higher standard of living, a plethora of consumer goods. It must be right. If there is a local organization that starts to branch out and then establishes counterparts in other areas of the country and, finally, becomes a national organization, then it is a better organization than it was before. It is doing something right—it is getting bigger. Bigger is more successful. Bigger is better than smaller. More is better than less.

"This church is growing." In other words, it is getting bigger. This is an interesting definition of "growth." In our country, growth means expansion. Growth does not mean depth. It doesn't mean wisdom, as in "growing 'in wisdom and stature'" (Luke 2:52). It means getting bigger.

Did Jesus gather twelve disciples around him because ten would have been too few? Given the performance of Judas, one could argue that twelve was one too many. Some might hold that Jesus could have stuck with Peter and let the rest go. Most of the group, you will remember, took off when it was time for the crucifixion. That's understandable. After all, they didn't sign up for failure.

A Side Trip

I arrive at a meeting. There are fourteen of us here. The host for the meeting says, "I thought there would be more coming. Well, that's too bad. We will try to do what we can, won't we? Maybe next time more will show up. Particularly if we get something off the ground."

How do I feel? That it wasn't important for me to come, but if five more had come I would be more important? Or is it the five who would be more important than the fourteen? Is anyone important? Is it true that if there are enough of us then all of us are important, but that if there aren't very many of us then none of us is important? How does that make you feel? It makes me feel rotten.

Another Side Trip

The A's and the Angels are playing. The pitcher for the A's is very famous. Fifty thousand fans turn out. The famous pitcher is awful that night. It is a terrible game. But it was a success, wasn't it? I mean, look how many people turned out. It was a lousy game. The score was nine to two, and there wasn't one exciting inning. But there were fifty thousand fans—you can't deny that. IT WAS A LOUSY GAME!

Have you ever been inspired by an hour's conversation with one person? Have you ever been bored to death by a supposedly fantastic speaker in a coliseum filled with people? Oh, yes, but what if 100,000 people had heard this one person who inspired you? If we could mass-produce that inspiration, put it on nationwide television in prime time—what an effect that would have!

Oh?

Did you ever feel you were doing something wrong that was right?

I Pay My Dues

"Church*man*"—a *man* who is faithful in church duties such as paying his pledge regularly, serving on church boards, attending services, and supporting the pastor.

A lot of it is a matter of motivation. Suppose you were a churchman because you wanted to be, or it came naturally to you, or you felt responsible to God, or something akin to any of the above. But if you are a success-oriented male, you are a churchman because that is what is expected of a successful man. It is like being one of the "elect": you don't know if you are of the "elect," but if you act as if you are, everyone will think that you probably are. If you are a success, then church people expect you to act that way, carry your load, pay your dues.

Minister: There are a lot of businessmen in my church. Thank God for them.

Friend: How do you mean?

M: They know how to get a job done. You can count on them when the every-member canvass is on, they will see that what you want goes through because they know how to move men, and they can sell the church to their friends.

F: Sounds like a good deal.

M: Of course, they always talk about running the church like a business.

F: Is that bad?

M: I thought so when I was in seminary, but now I don't. I think they are right. You have to run it like a business, or you won't survive.

The churchman who wants to be admired should do at least the following things:

1. Always take his family to church. The family that goes to church must be a fine family. Otherwise one kid would be driving his car around, another would be home in bed, and that would be a messed-up family. So they shall all go to church with him. And all look clean, and all be quiet.

2. Pay his pledge regularly. You may think that this is a matter between a man and his God, but you are wrong. The church secretary (or the church treasurer) knows if you pay your pledge regularly and how big it is. The word gets around. It is a good idea, in a church meeting, when someone is talking about a new project that needs financing, to offer to raise your pledge by a stated percentage each month. Others who want to be thought successful will follow suit. It helps if you don't pledge what you really could at the beginning of the fiscal year. Then you can raise it at times like this and look really impressive.

3. Assume the chairmanship of a board. It is well to

point out how busy you are, but to say that you realize that everyone needs to do his part and you will give it all you have. Besides, this gets you into the inner circle of the church, and you can move your weight around in a more acceptable way. You will discover that certain boards are prestigious and certain ones are not. "Finance" is prestigious; "Social Concerns" probably is not. The time will come when you will advance to the top lay job in the church and do your stint. Then you have arrived as a churchman.

4. Attend business meetings and make the crucial motions. Never make a motion unless you are certain that it will be passed by a large majority.

The rewards are pretty good for being a churchman. Even your wife thinks you can't be all bad if you are so active in the church and are looked up to by others. The women in the church will think you are great. "You do so much around here, I don't know what we would do without you." This helps in business, or whatever you do for a living, because your good reputation gets around to people who buy your product or make use of your services. A good reputation among the women of the church never hurt anyone.

But is this you? Do you really want to go to all those meetings, listen to the pastor week after week, do all the duties you should do in your church job and feel guilty because you know that so much more could be done? Is it enough to do this in order to be well thought of? Is that reward enough?

Motivation is a tricky thing—hard to sift, difficult to be certain of. Beware when men and women speak well of you and say all manner of nice things about you, for behind your back they are calling you a fool. But isn't it great to be a fool for Christ's sake? Is that why you are?

Be Present at Our Table, Lord

When I was in seminary, they taught us about the Deuteronomic view of history. This is the view of history in Deuteronomy, one of the duller biblical books. Simply stated it is that if you do right you will be rewarded with goodies, and if you do wrong you will be punished. When the Hebrew people followed God's law they prospered, and when they didn't things went from bad to worse. One of the great things about this view of history is that it is foolproof. When things are going well it is obvious that you are following God's will, and when things are going poorly it is likewise obvious that you are following some idol or fornicating or something. So, you see, it takes care of all eventualities.

Things haven't changed much, have they? People of my generation were brought up as Deuteronomists. We figured that if things were going well God was taking care of us. If things were going poorly, we were either being tested by God or else we had screwed up somewhere. We prayed, as we sat down to our bountiful meal, "Be present at our table, Lord, be here and everywhere adored." It's our food, but you gave it to us because we are good folks, Lord, and we pray to you and hope others do too. They certainly should, God knows.

If you are honest, thrifty, and industrious, God will reward you. You who are younger may think that I was a complete idiot to ever believe that, but I really did (and, to be excruciatingly honest, I still feel that way deep in my gut, though I have significant intellectual doubts). And if you are dishonest, spend money foolishly, and are lazy, God will get you. If not now, later. Just you wait and see.

This is the basic insight in "primitive" religion (the religion of preliterate peoples): you buy the god's favor by doing what is right. This has provided a pretty fair amount of the motivation for those of us in middle age to do what we were taught was right. If you do, the Lord rewards. And we know what the rewards are: a good job, a happy family, enough money to feel secure, and the respect of friends and acquaintances. As good Deuteronomists, we have discovered that when the job is in jeopardy, the family is falling apart, we aren't making much money, or folks don't look kindly on us anymore, we had better start praying harder, going to church more, or doing something that gets God back on our side. You see, in the world of my generation there is no such thing as chance, rough circumstances, or good honest failure. If we are suffering, *we have done something wrong* or *we have not done something right*. You can never really blame the economy, the President, the school system, the establishment, or anyone or anything other than yourself. We believe that each and every one of us ("My friends, as I address you this evening . . .") is responsible for his or her own life. You sow what you reap.

What a burden to carry. Each person completely and utterly responsible for himself. Not much interdependence there, and not much awareness of the complexity of life. "Why did God take my boy? What have I done wrong?" NOTHING, dammit, NOTHING. Could it be that it is not your fault?

I can understand why a lot of men committed suicide during the depression. They couldn't blame the country. It had to be them.

Do you think it was the writer of Deuteronomy who was resurrected and Jesus who died? How did that come out, anyway?

Get Them When They're Young

A successful religion is one which keeps the family intact. The church is to serve the family and keep it clean. There they are in the pew—father, mother, daughter, son—happy as larks to be in the Lord's house.

Our daughter seemed rather young to join the church—ten years old. But she wanted to. So I asked our pastor what he thought about it. He said that it was probably a good idea, because once they grow up they are often lost to the church. "Hang on to them while you can." So we let her join. If you get them when they're young, it may "take." Who knows?

For some reason the Sunday school (or "church school," as we are supposed to call it now—or is that already old-fashioned?) is supposed to function as a substitute parent, particularly in the areas of morals and Bible stories. The parents don't have to read Bible stories to the kids, because the teachers do that on

Sunday. Thank heaven! I got awfully tired of reading those things, anyway. And now that parents don't have to teach morals anymore, the Sunday school teacher can do that too. So when the kids come home and start telling us how we are supposed to live, we can nod and feel appreciative of what our kids are learning, and then do as we please, secure in the knowledge that the teachers at church are making up for what we no longer have to or care to do. It used to be that a man wasn't a success as a father unless he taught his children the basic moral facts of life—honesty, hard work, thriftiness, etc. But it is acceptable now to leave that to others. That is a load off our shoulders, isn't it?

The trouble is, of course, that the Sunday school teacher teaches morals but the kid learns how to live while he is at public school, when he is with his friends, and at home. The stuff he learns at church is useful when he is at church. However, church is basically for those who are into that sort of thing and for ministers' kids. If the church isn't your thing, well, there it is. My generation has a hard time with this one. At least, we do if we were brought up, as I was, in a Christian home. We never thought of the church as something that you either liked or didn't like. It was part of the fabric of society, part of growing up, and there wasn't really a choice. People went to church, and that was that. Kids did it and adults did it, and if you didn't do it, you were a little strange (or Jewish). The morals taught in Sunday school were the same as those taught at home (unless the teacher was awfully conservative or a wild-eyed liberal), and it was all one thing really—God,

America, home, church, family, doing right, and chicken dinners.

Middle-aged fathers, if they are religious, feel guilty about their kids and religion. Somehow the little devils don't seem to be too sold on religion. They can take it or leave it. They often think of it as an adult thing, and their job is to endure it if their parents are into it. Now I learned that kids are to be treated as human beings in their own right, so if my daughter doesn't want to go to church, she doesn't have to, does she? She is an O.K. person, and she has her reasons for not attending. But does that mean that I am supposed to teach her religion at home? My Lord, we haven't done that for years! Do people other than Mormons do that anymore? So we feel guilty and think we should be doing something we aren't doing and don't want to do, because we were used to drinking Christianity with the morning orange juice and don't understand why the kids don't too. It is very difficult to be a successful religious parent.

"Get them when they're young" sounds fine. But I don't think we've got them. Do you?

My Yoke Is Easy

There is a lot to be said for comfort. Lord knows, this world is chaotic at best, and everyone needs some rest. I would be the last one to knock the necessity of religion as a comforter.

"This world may be going to hell in a basket, but when I walk into that church on Sunday morning, I know that some things last."

"When I was in the hospital, I so missed the music. To sit in the sanctuary and hear that beautiful organ—it is like being in heaven."

"You get refreshed. We need it now more than ever. It makes your spirits brighten up. Charges me up for the week, you know what I mean?"

Yes, I know what you mean. There has to be a place, whether a church sanctuary or a kind of portable sanctuary that we carry around in our minds, where the stillness is and the comfort descends like a mantle. For it is not easy being on this planet at this time. The days are hypertensive. And his yoke is easy, and his burden is light (Matt. 11:30).

It is interesting, isn't it, that in our drive to succeed we need a place where we don't have to? A sanctuary where we can be passive and receive and just be there. A religion that represents stability and eternity. The drive to succeed is shifted into neutral.

I have sunk into the pew in Marble Collegiate in New York and have listened to Dr. Peale, and I have been to Sockman's church on Park Avenue, and I know what it means to feel that all is really right with the world after all. All has happened before, and all will happen again, and here we are and it is O.K. His yoke is easy and his burden is light.

But it is hard to separate the comfort from the American myth of success. Why do we feel comfortable? Because our pursuit of the success image is affirmed by the church—we are doing something right and God loves us for it? Because we will not be disturbed? Because no one will point out to us, in this passive, monological, organ music setting, that our families are disintegrating and our lives are falling apart? Are we comforted because God accepts us for what we are, or because he accepts us for the image we project? I am afraid that it is too often for the latter reason. The church doesn't want to "blow its cool" either; so it offers us comfort, for then it can survive. But the comfort comes at a price: the price of refusal to confront the realities of our lives—the hurts and the joys, the agonies and the ecstasies. If the church upset us, then we would blow our cool and lose control, and you can never be successful that way. You might say something you would be sorry for, you might step on someone's toes, you might upset the apple cart, and it would get out all over town, and then who knows what would happen?

Is comfort at the price of deception really comfort? Or is it rather a spiritual morphine, administered regularly in small doses (but large enough to get one addicted)? What we call comfort is a fantasy world. What we call a haven is Disneyland. And when we go to worship, we are "off to see the wizard."

But I know the feeling. Comfort at any price is often better than upping the old blood pressure. And it is so nice to sit down and rest and be fed—for a change—before getting back into the rat race again.

"I am come to set fire on the earth" (Luke 12:49). Must be a different Jesus.

A TRANSITIONAL INTERLUDE

Breaking the Bonds

Before we move to Part II, I feel the need for a transition. Thus I am including an essay which is intensely personal. What it really is is the description of a conversion experience. Take it as that, if you will: not as a conversion that I am coveting for all of you or suggesting that you experience, not as a model for being reborn, but a personal witness, testimony, or whatever word says it for you.

I would be less than honest if I did not share with you my deepest fear. For I have asked a lot of you who read this book. I have invited you to listen to my hostilities and my anxieties, my sermons and my moralisms, my attacks and my caricatures. At times you may have felt put down, scolded. At other times I hope you felt affirmed and even exhilarated that another human being knew what you know. But now I must share with you what really makes us one. I will use no dialogues, no A and B. I will not preach. Maybe I will not deal with you at all. But please listen, for I have something to confess. And perhaps you will know what it is and you will identify with me. Perhaps you won't. Will you listen?

I was told that I could be anything I wanted to be. I was told that if I tried hard enough I could be a success at anything I chose. And I was told that that was good.

I had some fears. I was afraid that I would be inadequate, afraid that I could not "make it" with girls, afraid that I would somehow "blow it" in a big way and would not be successful, would not "win," would not even grow up. But I was told not to believe those fears. They were phantoms, unreal, not to be given in to or even entertained for a moment. When the night crept in and I lay in my bed and all the fears like monsters headed for me and I cried out, I was only having a nightmare. It would go away and Mommy would comfort me and Daddy would keep me safe.

When I was angry with my mother or my father, I was told not to be angry. That was not me. I could not get angry. It would hurt people. I could not "blow up," so I almost hurt a friend with a fork—practically stabbed him in the neck I was so mad at him. But I felt so guilty—afraid of my own anger and what it could do. People in our family don't get angry. Christians don't get mad.

I did not love some people I was supposed to love because they were related to me. When I admitted this, I was told that it was not so. Of course I loved them. "Now, Billy, you know that you love Auntie." (I can't stand her, Mother!) And so what I felt was wrong, and what I didn't feel was right.

Now what is the fear, I mentioned earlier? This fear, so long buried and so long contained, did not surface until I was forty. Then on my new natal day a man said to me, "You are afraid that you cannot be you and still be loved." And I cried like a baby on the day of my birth. He asked, "Is it a good hurt or a bad hurt?" I said, "It is a good hurt." For the forty-year-old dam had broken, and the waters rushed out and broke down the barriers built by years and years of hiding, deceiving, producing guilt, and repressing. That was it: I was afraid that I could not be me—me with my hostility, my crying, my inadequacies, my weakness, my feelings— that if I was me, I would not be loved. By my mother or father or wife or kids or, most of all, by me.

The fear buried deep within is the fear of failure to be me. The fear that if I am who I am, I will not succeed; if I am who I am, I will not be accepted; if I am who I am, I cannot face me—get up the next morning and meet myself in the mirror. I believed that someone else had to live my life. If *I* lived it, then it would not work. But now I knew, the day the pit opened, that I had to quit letting someone else live my life. I had to be born again, or born for once, or start this day as the first day of the rest of my life.

The fear is that who I am is not acceptable to others, to me, or to God. To be able to face that fear head on, and then to say, "It may be true, but I am what I am, whatever," is what I am working on now—not as a project, not as something to be accomplished, but as a life. What you will read in the rest of this book is an account of some tentative gropings, some stabs in the dark, some ways of saying what it is like to begin to live in middle age. These are some ways of coping with the fear. The fear is still there, but now faced. The lion remains crouched, but I know his growl and I recognize his face. He is still fearful, but I know his name and can name him, and he grows progressively less fierce.

Thank you for listening. Do not be dismayed. For beneath the tears, believe me, behind the hurt, the anger, and the pain, there is, as Nietzsche said, "deep, deep joy."

I am glad I opened the door.

PART II

Notes Toward the Liberating of the American Male

This first essay deals with my experiences with young adults. I am saluting them as evidence of some significant change in this society. I may romanticize them a bit, but take this as the prerogative of a middle-aged man who sometimes wishes he were twenty again.

When Are You Going to Amount to Something?

In my generation, it was assumed that you would go to school, go to college if you could, then get a job and amount to something.

A: What's George doing?
B: He's with the bank.
A: Great. Doing well?
B: He's already in management and moving right along.
A: And only three years out of college—wonderful!
B: We're so proud of him.

Why is going that route better than dropping out of college, knocking around the country, doing what your impulses tell you to do? Because it is productive, that's why it is better. When you work in a bank, you are producing something. And when you are bumming around the country, you are acting immaturely and you aren't producing anything. Besides, bumming around is self-centered, and working in a bank is—well, it isn't so self-centered.

Oh?

Suppose you are knocking around the country. You are trying to find yourself. Which means finding out what you are to do with your life. Obviously you aren't doing anything with your life if you aren't working steadily. "Doing something with your life" means working, producing, accomplishing something—like building up a checking account and then a savings account, saving for a house, a car, whatever. That is "doing something with your life."

It has occurred to me that the present generation has not ingested all the above values. They have some of them. Many of them feel guilty that they are letting down their parents, but they don't really feel that they have let themselves down. And that is the key. If I had dropped out of college, I would have felt that I had let myself down, not just my folks. If you don't feel you have let yourself down, then in another generation the value of settling down and doing something with your life as soon as possible is gone—disappeared, over with. That value is dead. In fact, it is already dying and has died with many people.

We are moving into a time when amounting to something does not necessarily mean production. And it does not necessarily mean that there is a certain time frame that has to be slavishly followed. Living is more episodic. It is not so linear. We are living more in moments, weekends, in filling this time full now and not worrying so much about a year from now or what will happen next week. So why go through all this schooling in sequence? Why not try out some non-school moments? See how people live who aren't in school. Immerse yourself in a piece of the world and see what happens.

I don't see younger people making long-term commitments in terms of jobs. Vocation is more a style of living: "I will live my life, and what job I do is secondary." "I will do one job for a while, and when that palls I will find another." It isn't the job, it is the "life-style" that is important. And that life-style is to be honestly me, no subterfuge, no significant compromises (unless there is conscious decision to compromise), and no buying into the production-oriented life-style of an older generation.

Isn't this what is often being said today?

Interestingly, the life-style involves a deep concern for commitment to persons, and especially to one particular person. I know young men and women who are living together to see if their relationship is deep enough for a lifetime commitment. In order to test out the relationship, they say, they don't want to make the marriage commitment immediately. This is not necessarily because they don't take marriage seriously. Often, they claim, they take it very seriously. They say that they want to make sure before taking such a big step.

How self-centered is this thing of developing your own life-style and living it? Is that more self-centered than automatically buying into a life-style that is given with your generation, as I did? That is conformist, but is it less self-centered? The argument is often made that if we all "do our own thing" we will not care about other people. But I see a generation today that is terribly concerned about the quality of life, about the environment, and about injustice. More concerned by far than my generation. We wanted to make money and get a better job and amount to something. And we considered social justice something of a luxury and something to be worked on if we got around to it. But what was really needed was for everyone to join the middle class.

I suppose people still want to amount to something; but in their own eyes now—not by buying into one view or another automatically, by being programmed—so that life becomes an adventure of discovery instead of a living out of a predestined plan.

I wonder if God is still trying to find himself?

The rest of these essays are my attempts at trying out a new style of living. Maybe not so new for you, but new for me. I am not attempting to deal with all the issues raised in Part I. That would be too pat, too simple. Rather, I want to tell you of some of my discoveries. The worlds of job, home, and religion overlap for me. This will be evident. I desire wholeness, and this means overlapping and breaking down the compartments we create. But that is part of the rebirth experience, isn't it?

We Can't Make It

When you are in your forties, the realization comes to you that you will never "make it." Not that you won't achieve more success. You may go onward and upward. But there is no summit, because you are driven on by a goal that cannot be reached.

A psychologist once told me that I had a "ceiling unlimited" personality. That is, I felt that I could achieve anything, but I was never satisfied with my achievement. I could always go higher and higher. There is no end. Unlimited. That is frightening.

If there is no end, and we are never satisfied—there is no summit, no goal, no top which cannot be topped—why do we strive?

It is satisfying to strive. To feel exhilarated by the climb. To know that you are making it, though you will never fully make it.

Why is it fun to play a card game and win, even though you know that next time you may very well lose?

The striving peps you up if you have some successes.

But it is wearing, wearying. Because there is no top.

And, sometimes, when the world stops, and there is space and water and mountains and high trees, there seems to be no reason for going at all, but only for staying.

The immensity of climbing is dwarfed by the immensity of being. At the point of stillness, there is no reason for movement. And I could stay in the green shade forever.

Since there is no top, there is no reason to climb all the time, for the short rises, the hills, the slopes, will always be there.

Since there is no top, the valleys take on new meaning. They have a being too, a substance which is not fully determined by the mountaintop.

So, finally, at mid-season in my life, there is a meaning in valleys and in going down as well as up. A meaning to resting and being still. A meaning to doing absolutely—my God, is it possible?—absolutely *nothing*.

Failing Is Equalizing

One summer I spent two weeks walking the streets of New York City, looking for a job. I would get tired of going to employment agencies, answering ads in the paper, etc., and would sometimes walk down Forty-second Street, usually turning into some cheap movie house before too long. I found myself looking at people on the street and envying them ("They have a job and I don't"). They were somehow above me, and I really didn't think that they deserved it. I was one of the unemployed, and I didn't like it. It was the first time in my life that I realized that I was not necessarily "singled out" as a person who was all that different. I could be unemployed too, I could be walking the streets, looking for work. I wasn't so unique. It was both invigorating and frightening. Invigorating because I now knew something of what it meant to be equal with unemployed people—a new experience, a new insight. Frightening because I was used to privilege and I wondered if I could adjust to being like so many other people.

Not too long ago my wife had a very serious accident and almost died. I would walk around the hospital corridors and out into the parking lot, and would look at people and divide them in my mind into those who were experiencing what I was experiencing and those who were not. I envied those who were leading "normal" lives, and I felt very close to those who were going through agony, wondering if their husband, wife, son, or daughter would live. People would come to me and ask about my wife, and then they would tell me of some problem of theirs, some hurt they were experiencing, as if now I knew and would understand. I was no longer up there in the ranks of the privileged who did not know grief, whose lives had not been threatened by loss. And, again, it felt good and bad. Good because to identify with the sufferers is to feel that you are one with humanity and to realize that illness rather than health is really the norm. Bad because I was frightened—afraid that I could not handle it, could not fall from my privileged state and still keep myself together.

Now being unemployed for two weeks is not exactly a failure experience. But our society views unemployment as failing, and working as the right and good thing. And I experienced, though briefly, something of what failing in the eyes of many could mean. Experiencing grief is not exactly failing either, except that there is a myth in this society, akin to the myth of success, that the norm is good health and that in the families that are making it everyone is healthy and happy. So here too I was failing, in a sense, in that I was not part of a completely healthy family.

Failing is equalizing. You feel as if you are more fully a member of the human race, that all the hurts and fears and inadequacies of other human beings are yours also. And you realize that only a small minority are privileged to live above illness and the lack of at least meaningful work. This is an odd experience, but a helpful one.

It is no easy thing to be part of humanity when you had thought of yourself for so long as above most of them.

A: Your son has really done well for himself, hasn't he?

B: He's just one of us, a human being like you and me.

A: Oh, sure, but look where he is today. Really up there. Aren't you proud?

B: He does what he does, you and I do what we do.

A: Oh, come on, don't play Mr. Humble.

B: I'm not. I'm just stating a fact. Sure, I'm proud of him. But not because he has a high position. I'm proud of him because he is a fine person.

A: And successful.

Being me is a lot like being everyone else. I eat, drink, sleep, take medicine, and will die someday. Maybe soon, maybe a long time from now. I am no better than my neighbor who has less education, no better than my friend who has discovered that the disease he has will probably not be cured, no better than my old buddy from many years back who spent a couple of years in a mental hospital as a patient. That fact is hard to accept at times, but it is true.

Though I was told for so many years that I was different, I am not. That is freeing. I don't have to act as if I am better, to push the "privilege" thing, to parade the education. I can like watching football on TV, be bored with academic lectures, and enjoy feeding my begonias. I can be a slob and an intellectual, and one is no better than the other. (Have you ever been to a concert of classical music and been bored to death, and then pretended you liked it to the wife of a friend because you knew that she judged people by whether they were "cultured" or not? To hell with that! I'll take Sarah Vaughan over any operatic diva you could name any day of the week. I even enjoy some country music.)

"The Son of man came eating and drinking" (Matt. 11:19), and one thing that means to me is that he lived life like most people when it came to the basics. He said he had no place to lay his head and he complained about it, which says to me that he liked his sleep too. It would help if the scripture mentioned that Jesus went to the bathroom, but I suppose that sort of thing doesn't make the scripture. Too bad. I'm sure he did.

Fine Tuning

One of the ways to deal with the tensions caused by the dominance of the success myth is to "fine-tune" your life, that is, slow down and condition your personal environment to a greater extent. Take it easier, move a little more slowly through life, and take time to look at sunsets and star jasmine.

This is "technique time" and I want to share a few with you.

Lie down in your backyard (on something comfortable, like a hammock) and shut everything out of your mind except the sun and air, the breeze and birdsongs. Do that until you are tired of it. Then quit. Sometimes it takes ten minutes, sometimes two hours. You deserve it, however long it takes. But you don't have to prove anything to anyone. Just do it because you want to. Or if you don't want to, don't. I like to do it. Maybe you will enjoy it.

Turn down a demand that is made on your time. Someone tells you that you really should go to some meeting or other tomorrow evening. But you don't want to go: not because you had something else planned, or because you can really, in any significant sense, justify not going—except that you plain don't want to go. Perhaps you don't enjoy the people who will be at the meeting, or it might be upsetting and your week has been tough enough, or you get tired of doing what people ask you to do. So don't go. Guilt may come. But after you have done this a few times, the guilt gets less and less. In fact, some good old-fashioned self-righteousness creeps in. "Hey, I can do what I want to do and like it." I look at it this way: in my work, I meet a lot of demands. Why should I succumb to demands outside my work when I can turn them down and feel fine?

Admit to yourself that you genuinely enjoy washing the dishes, sweeping the floor, or cooking breakfast—even if that is your wife's role—and go ahead and do it. Volunteer? Why not? There is a sense of accomplishment that comes from washing dishes. I am of the opinion that I wash a dish cleaner than does my wife. Of course, I don't do it as often, so I take more pride in it. If it were my normal job, I would probably hate it. But it isn't, so why not do it once in a while?

One of the great things about modern cars is that you can close the windows and it is quiet inside. You can drive along with the windows closed and the radio on (playing music you really like, not what you are supposed to like) and be oblivious to everything else. If it is hot and you have air conditioning, that is even better. Then the noise of the fan shuts out the outside world. I can think of all sorts of excuses, even legitimate rationalizations, for driving somewhere by myself. And with a fifty-five-mile speed limit, it takes even longer. Beautiful!

The great thing about being over forty is that I do not have to spend as much time justifying my existence to myself. No longer do I honestly believe that I am going to have a lot of effect on the world. No longer do I think of myself as indispensable in every job I do or office I hold. The world can go along almost as well if I stay in bed for a couple of extra hours. When I am on vacation, things still get done (there are other people who do things too, and reasonably well on occasion). So I don't worry so much about being selfish. As an over-forty friend of mine said the other day, "Now I do pretty much what I want to do." He was talking primarily about what he does after working hours (though he enjoys his job). What I would say is that since I am basically a useful person in terms of my work and my relationship with others, I feel free to do a lot of things that are of no use at all except that they give me pleasure. It is a matter of figuring that you deserve to be selfish once in a while because you have paid your dues. But it isn't really "selfish." That puts a value judgment on it which is negative. It is a matter of centering on yourself and being honest about your own feelings. It is also true that when you are over forty you have a better idea of what you enjoy doing. A lot of possibilities have been discarded. You have tried some things and like them and want to do them more often—making love, working in the garden, frying eggs, or whatever. Being freed from having to justify my existence, from having a useful purpose for all my actions, enables me to do more fine-tuning of my personal environment.

My Job Is a Job

Ex-pastors are an interesting group. Not long ago, I had occasion to be with a group of them, and one of the flashes of insight that came to one as he was recuperating from his stint in the pastorate was that a job, even the job of being a pastor, is *a job*, and doesn't have to be one's whole life. He was in a regular job now, and he saw it as a job and could handle it and not let it run him. But when he was a pastor, that pretty much defined him.

A job is something that can happen *to* you as well as something that you make happen. When I see a job as something I have to make happen or it doesn't have any existence at all, I am hooked. But when my job can also just happen to me—be there when I go to the office and happen for a day, and then not happen after I come home—then I am free *from* it, and, on the next day, *for* it. The older I get, the more I have to be able to take my job and leave it alone. I am sure that it is noble to think of one's job as a "calling." But the danger in that is that a "calling" gets wrapped up with guilt when I am not doing a fantastic piece of work or when I resent aspects of the job that have never thrilled me. And if it is a job, a good job, but not the be-all and end-all of existence, then I can gain perspective on it, can look at it over there as well as right here and say, "Hey, there's my job—hello—good-bye."

Part of the trick of treating a job as a job is arriving at the stage in your development when you are a professional; for example, when I preach. Now I don't take thirty hours to put a sermon together (actually I never did, but that sounds as if maybe I did and looks impressive), but I know how to do it and how to deliver it, and it generally comes off well. I am now a professional when it comes to preaching, so I am better able to look at it as a job—to salute it and leave it, to sweat it when I need to and not to sweat it when I don't. A professional should be able to relax. Don't you think so? When you do something well because you know how to do it and have known how to do it for a reasonable length of time, you can be free of it. Now I know that you can always do a job better, no matter how often you have done it well. But then you can get back on the success treadmill so easily. You begin to refine the product so that the subtleties are more important than the essence of the product. You sweat the subtleties, and die of a heart attack. Besides, look at it this way: you can do the job reasonably well and people affirm your doing of it—why not relax with it and go on to something else that you don't do so well and work on that if you want a challenge?

Since my job is my way of producing, and production helps to define me, I need to produce in areas which are really me. In order to do that, I need to be professional enough in enough areas not to have to be bound to a success I have already reached, so as to be able to try some areas in which I haven't produced. But not necessarily on the job. People in their middle years can get so good at their jobs that they have to add on jobs to feel useful. But if you are good at your job, why not add on in areas not related to your job? Like gardening or hiking or reading history. Something that has nothing to do with your job and gives you a sense of accomplishment, but not something that a host of people judge you on. A job is a job—but it doesn't define you.

There is a confidence born of competence that is not to be underrated. It is one of the deep joys of the middle years—not to be pushing it all the time, but to know that you do do some things well, really well. There are times when that is enough to give you a tranquil sleep. Just that: a quiet competence, and then—goodnight.

Whose Family Is It?

My family is not my most prized possession.

I don't own my family. It isn't—they aren't—*my* family.

What happens is that we are given the privilege, the experience, the gift, of living with some people who are known as wife, son, daughter. In the case of sons and daughters we live with them for a relatively short period of time. Hopefully, you and I live with the person known as wife for a longer period. But it is the living with them that is the gift. It isn't that they are gifts to us in the sense that we can own them.

It is easier to live with the folks in your house if you realize that most of the problems you have with them are *your* problems, not theirs. I overreact to daughter when she does something I don't like. My overreaction is probably because I seldom got angry when I was a child—at least at home. And so I am making up for it by getting inappropriately angry in my middle age. Daughter was the stimulus to my anger, but my anger comes from much deeper roots. I am partly angry at her, and to a great extent I am getting a kick out of being angry. Hitting something or someone sometimes helps me get higher on my anger. Did you ever get angry at someone and discover that that someone was falsely accused? He or she didn't do it. And you felt cheated. All that great anger gone to waste. Well, maybe it helped you.

Me: Why did you drop that glass?
She: It was slippery. It wasn't my fault.
Me: If it wasn't your fault, then whose fault was it? It certainly wasn't mine.
She: Why does it always have to be someone's fault? I dropped the glass. I didn't want to do it, but I did it. So what's so big about that?
Me: Don't ever do it again! Ever!
She: Sure, Dad, sure.

Why does it have to be someone's fault? Do I need to punish someone? Why do I need to? You see, it is my problem. She isn't into the "fault-finding" business at all. I am. She dropped a glass. It broke. She isn't happy about it, but it happened. Why can't I leave it at that?

When I recognize that it is my problem and not something strange about daughter, son, or wife, then it helps, because I can live with me, and I can do something about my reactions. So it is mainly me I have to live with. I can be a little more relaxed about them.

It is also easier to live with the people in your house if you don't take them too seriously. We who are professionals in human relationships tend to take relationships in the home very seriously. What wife says is so significant—it tells something about our relationship. How son is feeling is very important—he is growing up and is discovering life. O.K. But wife says a lot of dumb things, and most of what she says isn't all that important, even if it sounds that way. And the same with me. It doesn't have to be important to be listened to. Have you ever caught yourself telling wife about your day and what happened to you and all of a sudden you realize that you are boring her? Then you shut up. Why not continue? After all, you have to listen to some garbage from her once in a while too. Don't be so serious about how you are affecting her. You like to hear yourself talk, and that has something to say for it. So she is bored. So what? Or when daughter is talking about boys and how she feels about them. This may strike you as the time to deal seriously with male-female relationships. Why not just listen to her tell you about boys? She wants to talk to someone, and you are the nearest someone. But it isn't so dead serious.

The family with whom it is my privilege to live allow me to be me—often more than I realize. They know me, and they usually know me better than I know me. They are more forgiving, more understanding, more tolerant, more aware of me than I am. So enjoy! I can actually be me with all my faults and still be accepted by them. The least I can do is give them the same gift: I can be me and let them be them. It is when we try to change each other that we get into trouble.

I try to change people in order to control them, in order to mold them into someone who does not threaten me or to whom I can adjust with a minimum of effort. But that is a losing battle. I underestimate my ability to deal with them as they are. I don't have to change them or control them; I can adjust to them with minimum, medium, or maximum effort. If it takes maximum effort for me to adjust to them, it is the same with them. Most of us don't have the strength for it. So we ignore, or in some way write off, those with whom it takes too much effort to adjust, and we stick with the easier ones. But what if the folks in our house are hard to adjust to? My feeling is that we find it hard to adjust to them because we are trying to change them. It is a vicious circle. You try to change a person because it requires too much of you to deal with him as he is, but when you try to change him, much more is required of you and he is harder to deal with. It is probably better to tolerate him, since he is tolerating you. Don't try to change him, and your adjustment to him will come easier over a period of time.

I have found that the gift of other people in the home is a fantastic one. At times it is just plain fascinating to watch these people live. To have a son's world open up to me: he sees things, and thinks thoughts that are new to me. To hear a wife tell you what it is to be a woman in our society. Wild! And to see a daughter develop a sensitivity for what I would otherwise ignore. This is a gift that is easier to enjoy in middle age. Now I have more time for it. I am not trying to move higher and higher up the ladder of job success. I can listen to these folks and enjoy their living. They are quite interesting people, once I let go of them, don't claim them for my own, and live *with* instead of *over* them.

Whose family is it? Perhaps it is God's. It certainly isn't mine.

Joy Is like the Rain

Remember the movies about what it is really like when you meet the right girl? Joy, pure joy. A little pain, perhaps, but then the kiss. And the heavens open up. She is the one. You are "Mr. Right." You get married and live happily ever after.

In all our male childhood fantasies, this was it. The looking around. The finding. The passion. The aftermath of joy abounding. Marriage would be one long orgasm. Rolling, pounding surf, for ever and ever, Amen.

On days when you don't really want to get up, it is
     raining.
The sky is gray, sullen.
The wet stuff keeps coming down.
The coffee tastes like it.
     So does the toast.
She never looks like much when she gets up anyway.
     Today she looks worse.
But the eggs are great.
And the rain?
     We needed it.
But not all this. Not all the grayness.
     Not all the murk.

Joy is like the rain.

Joy is the eggs tasting great when the rest of the
     breakfast is lousy.

Joy is holding hands after a fight.
Joy is having a job to go to even if you couldn't
perform in bed this morning.

Joy is like the rain.

Joy is in bits, moments, washing you clean.
    Though you know you will get dirty again.
Joy is the sun breaking through, though there are
    four more months of winter.
Joy is saying something to someone else,
    and it was appreciated.

All our fantasies about joy are fantasy. We live
happily ever after—once in a while. There is no "Mr.
Right" or "Mr. Wrong." There is no "she is THE ONE
for me." Marriages are not made in heaven, but on
earth.

Jesus, remember, had a fantastic time with Mary and
Martha and in one week he was dead. That was joy, and
he knew it.

Walt Disney was just about right, though the balance
was a bit off. In a Disney movie, you always knew that
if you had had ten minutes of everything going great,
there would be five minutes of fear, possibly even
death, or at least something gone wrong. But it would
all come out fine. It seems to me that reality is ten
minutes of things going wrong, ten minutes of in-
between, and a minute and a half of pure joy.

As for the ending—not happy, not necessarily sad,
but, hopefully, worth it.

From Man to Person

In a way, it is too bad that the term "man" no longer means what it once did. When "man" meant humanity, there was a lot to be said for using it: "We are all in the family of man"—that sort of thing. But now it has been genderized, and it means males. So we have to move from thinking exclusively about male or female and think instead about persons.

Why?

Because the connotation of "man" is "a real man," "a man's man," a "he-man," not just a male person. Then there is the hang-up about homosexuality. No homosexual male can be a man: he has to be a "faggot" or a "queer"—but not a man. The only way to overcome this thing in terms of language it seems, is to call men and women "persons."

This has been a trip for me—from Betty Friedan to Germaine Greer to now. When I read *The Feminine Mystique* it was as if the veil had been lifted from my eyes. I showed it to my wife. She read it and went out and got a job. Talk about the power of the pen! Then later I read *The Female Eunuch* and understood how bound I was to male images of men and women. Beautiful books, particularly for men.

When I am with women who are into the women's movement and I sit with them through a lecture by a man who speaks of "men" or "man" when he means both sexes, I sit there and agonize. Partly because I am afraid that one of my women friends is going to stand up and make a speech about sexist language, and I hate confrontation, and partly because I feel personally that the women are being put down and they are persons like me and I resent being put down. Is it so difficult to say "he and she," or to say "persons" instead of "man"? It gets a lot easier the more you do it.

It is freeing to think of yourself primarily as a person and secondarily as male. You feel a lot closer to a much wider variety of people—particularly to people who are "gay" or bisexual, but also to people who are heterosexual but feeling-oriented (if males) or aggressive (if females). You don't have to put up with this nonsense about men not crying or hugging other men. And you don't have to feel defensive around aggressive women. We are all persons, and some persons cry, some hug, some dominate, some do a lot of things that are very human much more than they are male or female.

I think this is what St. Paul meant by "neither male nor female" (Gal. 3:28). He didn't mean that there weren't men and women; he meant that that wasn't the main thing. The main thing is that we are persons and that God can love us and we can care for, with, and about each other. You could berate Jesus for not being married, or not engaging in sexual intercourse (as D. H. Lawrence did), but I am rather glad that he chose not to be like most men. He wasn't "gay," but he was single. He didn't push celibacy, but as far as we know he didn't have intercourse. He was a person who lived his life-style, and that was his thing to do at that time. He was first of all a person and secondarily a man. All this business about painting Jesus so he looks more "masculine" or selecting the scripture passages which bring out his "machismo" is rather ridiculous. He was who he was, and let's not make him into someone who compensates for our lacks or who fits into our images.

If I am a person and you are a person, then we aren't only "brothers" and "sisters." We are human beings. "Hello, person." "Hello, human being." The Friends knew what they were doing. They used to (maybe still do) call each other by their full names. If I were greeted by a Friend, I would be greeted as William Lacy Malcomson, middle name and all. Not as "Brother Bill," but with no title, no modifier. Just me. It takes a couple more syllables, but it is worth it.

A Failure Faith

Wouldn't it be nice if a good old American religion like Christianity were geared to success? After all, we would all appreciate peace of mind, peace of soul, power, victory, winning, and a God who brings all these goodies at Christmas (or Easter, because that is when more Christians are together). But Christianity, which is not, of course, a good old American religion at all, is for failures.

"No cross, no crown."

No "cheap grace."

"In the world ye shall have tribulation" (John 16:33).

Imagine this dialogue:

A: Hey, man, you really ought to try Jesus.

B: Why?

A: He carried a cross, and if you follow him you might get knocked around a bit too.

B: Oh?

A: Yeah. And he never promised that things would be rosy. He said that trouble was the normal thing.

B: Fantastic!

A: And you have to forgive your brother to really receive forgiveness yourself.

B: Terrific!

A: You can't be certain of much of anything, and you can bring down upon yourself the wrath of a lot of people whose favor you want.

B: I'll try him, I'll try him.

Can you imagine such a dialogue?

Get this picture: People pouring into a church with expectancy on their faces. The first hymn, the hymn of celebration, is:

> Jesus walked this lonesome valley;
> He had to walk it by himself.
> Oh, nobody else could walk it for him;
> He had to walk it by himself.
>
> We must walk this lonesome valley;
> We have to walk it by ourselves;
> Oh, nobody else can walk it for us;
> We have to walk it by ourselves.

Wouldn't that send them out rejoicing?
It would?

It should.

Why?

Because the American myth that success is the norm is pure fantasy—or impure farce. Failure, not success, is the norm. And this is all right. It isn't wrong, it is all right.

The majority of people do not make a success of their lives. Most of them, to paraphrase the words of T. S. Eliot, measure out their lives with coffee spoons. Most people are sad, or in neutral, more than they are happy. We simply do not live as the TV situation comedies say we should live. They are a lie. We do not live as characters lived in the syrupy movies of the forties and fifties. They were a lie too.

One summer when I was in college, I was an elevator operator on the Upper West Side of New York City. On a particular day, a fellow operator and I were talking about our jobs. I hated mine; he had no love for his either. He said, "Well, most people don't like their jobs—right?" I was young and I thought, "He has to be wrong." I don't think he was, now. I think he was dead right. There are a few of us privileged types who have had a lot of education, the "right" parents, and a good many breaks along the way, who happen to be in jobs we enjoy. But we are in the minority.

Jesus won't bring you success, fella. You can walk down every sawdust trail in this nation, get converted over and over again, sing "Praise God" every five minutes, and you can still fail miserably. Any evangelist who tells you that Jesus brings success is a charlatan.

Sure, Jesus can help you overcome drugs. Sure, Jesus can help you overcome your drinking problem. Sure, Jesus can help your marriage. But once you have dealt with these matters, your whole life is right out there in front of you, full of other kinds of failures.

I have a friend who was in prison for nine years of his life. He lived for the moment when he could be released. He made it. Success! Freedom! Wow, man! Then he got into drugs, smashed up his car, and has been in and out of jail again. He is out of prison now, to be sure. He probably will not go in again. He has a fine wife. But he will never achieve the American dream of success. He will be a failure who adjusts to his failing, over and over and over again.

Jesus can help you over spectacular hurdles, and forgive you for colossal sins, but most of what Jesus really does is to help you make it through the average normal day of mostly failure, some success.

It isn't a bad religion, on the whole.

That's God's Problem

This could very well be a "cop-out," but such things don't worry me as much as they used to. (I used to think that there was a little person resting on my shoulder who every time I did something a little less heroic than what I might be doing whispered, "That's a cop-out." He stopped whispering when I hit forty.) Some things are my problem, but an increasing number of things are God's problem.

Seeing that the kids have good food, decent clothes,

and an interesting father is my problem. Whether or not any one of them will die in an accident or acquire some incurable disease or encounter some terrible disaster is God's problem. Dealing with my feelings and making some sense of my life is my problem. When I die or what happens to me after death is God's problem.

Do you see what I am driving at? There are some things I can control and some I cannot. There are some things it makes sense to worry about because I can do something about them. There are some things it is useless to worry about because I can do nothing about them. It is like watching the Dow-Jones average and worrying about how much farther down your mutual-fund stock is going to go and then realizing that you could take a risk and redeem it or you could leave it in and who knows what will happen. Then you realize that, however much you worry, you won't affect the stock market. Your money is your problem, but the stock market is God's problem.

It helps a lot to dump things on God—or, if you prefer, to cast your burdens on the Lord (I prefer my phrase).

"Lord, I know that you have a lot on your mind. God knows, it isn't easy, running this world. I have a lot on my mind too. How about my pushing some of what is on my mind off on you, because I am frustrated. I have learned that there are so many things which I cannot control, so many problems which I cannot begin to solve. I don't know if you can deal with them or not, but I would rather you worried about them than I. I figure that since you are so much bigger and more all-encompassing than I am, you can deal with more than I can. So go to it and good luck. I've had it."

A lot of praying is dumping things on God, and I have done more of it in my middle years. The difference is that now I know what can be dumped on God and what I have to do myself. This comes with maturity. I don't dump stupid, inconsequential things on God anymore; I just give him the big stuff. I dump a friend's terminal illness on him, but not my worry about getting this book done. It is a matter of the great and the small, the overwhelming and the manageable. Isn't this faith?— faith in a God who deals with the overwhelming. I know—you can say that God works in all things and that he is in the small and the large. Every hair on our heads is numbered, and no sparrow falls without his knowing it and all that. O.K. But I take that kind of thing, even if it is scriptural, as romantic hyperbole. It is useful exaggeration in that it is a way of saying that God cares about all of us. But my view is that God has a lot more important things to do than to care about the hairs on my head. That is my problem, not his. In fact, I think we trivialize God too much. We assume that he cares whether we take flight 407 or flight 416. I care about that, but my belief is that God couldn't care less. If he is going to worry about all the big things, the least I can do is take the mundane matters of my life off his back. I suppose it makes some sense to say that he is in all the little things of my life; however, I don't think of him as being involved in a direct way, but only in a general way. Otherwise, we get into this automaton thing where God moves us around as if we were machines. That doesn't wash with me. God is too big for that. If he had wanted machines instead of people, he would have created them and left us alone.

I really believe that we do a lot on our own and that God leaves most of the day-to-day details of our lives up to us. We can "make it" or "blow it," and whichever way we go often makes little or no difference to him. He is about such matters as eco-justice and the agonies of the dying. Of course, so are we, but in small ways. I think that we have a right to privacy, and so does he. We can hide from him and go our own ways, and he can be shut of us from time to time; but we also need to check in and keep contact—and so does he. However, I refuse to take as seriously as I used to the times when I feel separated from God. I can make the connection again if I want to. I don't have to wallow in all that existential mire. And if he really wants me, he can break through.

In a room where I used to sleep, there was a plaque on the wall that somehow communicated to me the idea that God was watching all that I did. I don't think that anymore—and it is freeing. To feel as if you are being watched by God is religious paranoia. It has the same effect as any paranoia: defensiveness, fear, overreaction. But, you see, I have my problems and God has his. I am welcome to mine and he to his. I don't have to be him, nor he me. That isn't a bad arrangement.

Sin and Success

One of the most deeply held convictions of the Christian faith is that persons are sinners. We go against our own best interests a good deal of the time, we do what will harm others rather than what will contribute to their well-being, and this is what we should expect. This is not to say that we do wrong acts most of the time, or that we are dreadful persons, or that we are doomed to hell and that's it. But the good old Christian understanding of sin and its pervasiveness helps us out when we are moving toward romanticism regarding human nature.

Our nation has moved through the trauma known as Watergate. One of the disturbing things about this period in our history is that a lot of sin-ignoring self-righteousness was rampant: "President Nixon and his crowd were people who did bad things, and they should be punished"—the assumption being that then we could get people in office who would do good things. But it seems to me that that is not the point. An orgy of self-righteousness is even more disgusting than an orgy of sin.

"You are bad persons. We need to get rid of you so that good people can take over. People like us. If we were in your shoes, we would never do what you did, or even think of it."

Really?

Come, now.

The point is not to replace bad people with good people. We are all about equal with each other on this one. Once in a while a demonic person like Hitler comes along, but, thank God, such people are rare. What we need is checks and balances, so that when people do things that hurt the public good, they can be caught up short and checkmated. In fact, the American system assumes the fact of sin, and that is basically why there are checks and balances. Watergate is a shining example of the validity of the American way of governing. It recognizes sin and does something about it.

But somehow we want to succeed in overcoming badness and to replace it with goodness, so that we won't have to worry anymore. Or, we wish that were possible. Every time we elect a person to office, we hope that he or she will be a good person. "I vote for the man, not the party." But we are also highly critical of our elected official when he or she does something "wrong." We say, "That's a politician for you." In other words, we recognize sin, and deep down we expect people to be that way. But we hope against hope that some folks will rise above it all. They don't. And we don't.

The point is, don't give anyone (including me and you, brothers and sisters) too much power. Always have a check, an over-against which can deter the person from taking upon him or herself too much authority. It is a funny thing about us sinners. We can balance each other out.

Trust the Weak

Not very many years ago in this nation there was a big controversy over a vice-presidential candidate. It seems that he had undergone psychiatric care a couple of times, and there was a strong feeling on the part of

many Americans that to have done this indicated that
he might not be fit for the vice-presidency—particularly
if he had to succeed the President upon the occasion of
the latter's death.

A: What do you think of Peter as the head of the
church?
B: You don't mean that you are seriously considering
him, do you?
A: Why not?
B: Well, after all, he did deny our Lord, you know.
A: Sure, but our Lord forgave him.
B: Yes, but you can't count on a man like that. If he
does something like that once, he might very well do
it again.
A: Do you think so?
B: Yes. And, besides, he is so impetuous. He's liable to
say just about anything that comes into his head.
You know the problems the churches have had with
him on that score.
A: At least he is honest. I mean, he says what he
thinks.
B: That's all right for the run-of-the-mill apostle, but
when you are talking about the head of the church,
you have to be more selective.
A: I think Peter is only human.
B: That's my point.

I have a friend who spent a good deal of time in a
mental hospital. He was a patient. He had the best of
care and is now functioning in "normal" society. He is a

minister by profession. He is well aware of what happened to him, and he knows that he continually has to monitor his feelings. But he is actually a much healthier person than he used to be—more mature, more aware of who he is. And he is also more compassionate. He knows what it is to "go through it." Would you hire him as your pastor?

It is that old devil the myth again—the myth that you can only trust the strong. After all, in a high leadership position you need people who are almost superhuman. Don't you? Do you? Why? Perhaps you need someone who is very human, who is aware of who he is, with his failings, his problems, his needs, his inadequacies. Remember how many people in this country reacted to Adlai Stevenson when he ran for the presidency: "He is indecisive, he can't make up his mind." I wonder if he was weighing the alternatives? Is that so awful? Harry Truman was anything but indecisive, and he gave orders to drop two atomic bombs. We are still arguing over whether both were needed, or even one of them.

We want gods to lead us—is that it? We are afraid of leaders who are human. Our leaders are to be upon pedestals and are not to admit mistakes. They are to be all-knowing, all-wise. Not like us. Or, rather, as we wish we were, or think we could be if only we were given the chance.

Have we forgotten the Old Testament? Even God made mistakes there. He would actually repent of some of his actions. Ridiculous! There is no hope if God isn't perfect—right?

How about a slogan right here. "Trust the Weak." Or, perhaps, "Follow the Failures." Would that make a good bumper sticker? Would you put it on your car?

Let us say that the university catalog has listed this course title: "How to Be a Leader, Though Human, and Get People to Like It." It might do a lot to kill the savior myth. Let's put to rest the myth that leaders must be superhuman, above fear, inadequacy, failure, stress, and disease.

I would vote for Peter for head of the church any day.

I Don't Worry About What Other People Think

A number of years ago I was sitting on the porch of an inn with a woman who was fifty-five years old or thereabouts. We were chatting about this and that, waxing philosophical as the evening wore on. At one point she said something that I have thought about a lot since then: "You know, Bill, I am now at the age where I really don't care as much as I used to about what other people think of me."

I wondered at the time if that sort of feeling came with middle age or later, because this has been a problem of mine (and of my generation) for a long time. We have been taught to care a great deal about what other people think of us. In fact, one of the major keys to success is to live your life in such a way that other people think very highly of you and don't have occasion to think badly of you. You try to avoid doing anything that might antagonize people whose approval you need in order to move ahead. But I have always been envious of people who told me (and I often wondered if they were lying or engaging in wishful thinking) that they didn't worry about what other people thought of them.

Now that I am into the middle years of my life, I can testify to the fact that I no longer worry *as much* about what other people think. For me this can be very specific in that I know now that some people do not like me and I also know that I can handle this. I can do so because I know that their dislike is due in some cases to stands I have taken that I feel are right and in other cases to a personality conflict. In other words, if I can justify their not liking me, I feel relatively good about it. It used to be that whatever the reason might be, justified or not, I couldn't stand it if I knew that certain people didn't like me. So that is an improvement.

But why is it that I can handle the problem better now? Does something come automatically with age? Not automatically, but something can come, and that something is inner security, the awareness that who I am is all right, and, in fact, really pretty good. I am more confident about who I am, more personally secure, so that when I do things or say things or live in such a way that I antagonize or turn off some people, I know now that it is me who is being this way and that I like the me who is this way. The problems that some other people might have with me are their problems, not mine. I have accepted the fact that not everyone is going to like me. And that is fine. At least it is the *real* me whom they do not like. And at least *I* like me.

A problem with this for religious types is that we have been taught that Christians are supposed to love everyone. This gets translated as liking everyone, and that gets translated as feeling guilty (it is my fault and it is bad) when we admit to ourselves that we don't like everyone. But look at Jesus. You can't convince me that Jesus liked most of the Pharisees. He cared about them in that he told them off and didn't ignore them, but I don't believe that he liked them. Somehow Jesus seems to have known the difference between caring and liking. And for me this is where it is at.

Caring for someone is possible even when you don't like the person. I have inquired about the health of people whom I do not like, I have sent sympathy cards to people I can't stand, and I have worked hard to find a job for folks whose personalities grate on me. Finally, I have discovered that you can work with people and for people whom you do not like and that is all right.

Again, it is a matter of inner security, isn't it? My dislike of some people is *my* dislike of them. It is a genuine feeling. It is really me who is doing the disliking. And I have a valid reason for it. They rub me the wrong way, remind me of someone I didn't like in the past, are personally obnoxious, or whatever. My feelings of dislike are me and are valid. And it does no good to feel guilty about these feelings as if they represented a bad side of me or an unconverted or unchristian aspect of my personality.

All this may strike you as being of small consequence. But it is of great consequence to many of us. To have been so caught up in the insecurity of wondering if certain folks like us or not, of trying to make everyone like us, of feeling guilty when we were rejected or disliked, and then to begin to feel free of this anxiety, is a very cleansing experience. Don't minimize it. For some of us, freedom has been bought at a price, and we prize that freedom because it looks so good in contrast to the bondage we once knew.

Putting Down Roots

One of the problems with the desire for success is that there is always another bridge to cross, another mountain to climb, another program to develop and see through to its conclusion, and another and another and another, without end. It is time to put down roots.

But if you put down roots, you get stale, don't you? "Put down roots and you go to seed. No challenge. You will stay in the same old rut—mark my words."

There is enough variety in the average backyard to keep you busy for the rest of your life.

If you studied one human life, you would never get bored.

Or if you and I worked on one idea for as much as ten years, it could keep us significantly occupied.

Really?

We worship size. Get involved in bigger, better, and more, and give all you have until you drop and die.

"Died in harness, didn't he? By God, that's the way to go!"
"Died with his boots on—what a man he was!"

Is it better to wear out than to wear down?
There are times when I think that the most

significant life is lived by the person who has a terminal illness. He lives each day as if it were his last, and lives it to the fullest. And he doesn't have to accomplish anything that day except to get through it with dignity.

It is difficult to look directly at a person when you are climbing over him on your way to the top. But what if you don't want to get to the top? What if you wanted to look at this person and have him look at you? Look deep within. Would that be worth a day of your time?

I am now at the stage in my life where I want to put down roots. I like my job. I like the people with whom I work. I like my house, my neighborhood, my community. We could grow here and live out our years in meaningful ways. There is enough variety, enough creative potential in my work, family, community, to keep me from getting bored. Enough challenge in one day. From outside of me and from within me.

(I keep telling myself.)

Putting down roots means growing in depth, not in breadth. I suppose I know a lot, but I need time to concentrate on what is significant knowledge—to make some judgments. There are a lot of things I do well—but I need to upgrade myself in what I do best.

(Still talking to myself.)

It is better to pace myself and be proud of my ability to make a ten-mile hike in the high Sierras than it is to run a company. It is more important to be a part of the life of my daughter than it is to be recognized in a crowd. It is better for me to be taken seriously by my faculty colleagues than it is to write a best seller.

(If I keep this up, I may believe it.)

When you turn down the volume, you hear more.

When you walk more slowly, you can see the trees, one by one.

When you kneel by the brook, you can count the stones and the leaves, and, if you look very, very closely, the drops of water.

Thoreau was no dummy.

AN EPILOGUE

From Bondage to Freedom

It is basically a matter of breaking the bonds that enslave us. These bonds are the images that determine our lives: the images of masculinity, of producer, of performer. It is the images that have to die. Without death, there is no resurrection.

Sometimes it takes a conversion experience, as it did with me, a plunge to the bottom and a rising toward the sun, in order for the bonds to be broken. In reality, there are usually a series of such experiences: times when you met people who helped to free you, and other times when you happened to be in the right place at the right time and something happened that opened a new door.

The resurrection is a process of resurrecting, of experiencing new life. The freedom is a freeing—again, a process of finding out what it means to be free of some images but not all, to have some bonds broken but others holding fast. There is no pinnacle of success in the process of freeing. But it has its moments, and the moments are worth all the striving.

There is a danger in smuggling in a new image—the image of freedom or of liberation. The liberation of the American male could become a goal, but it could become a binding image, particularly if it gets too clearly defined. I hope that I have been aware of that danger in this book. I do not want to define this goal, or, rather, this process. All I can do is attest to my experiences, my moments of freeing. I have no panaceas, no formulas that are certain to work, and no list of testimonial letters. All I know is that whereas before I was blinded to some possibilities, now I can see more clearly the road ahead for me. I know that I was lost in a lot of blind alleys that led me to more and more grieving, and now I am finding some hope and some joy, and that is good. Why this is happening I am not sure. There are a lot of factors I could list, but no one factor, is key, except, possibly, the flash of insight received in the words "You are afraid that you cannot be you and still be loved."

The faith I have is that God's grace is not a myth but a reality. The song title "Amazing Grace" does say it. It is amazing, because mysterious and uncontrollable. Amazing because it comes when it wishes and goes for no reason. Amazing because I cannot label it or put it on a wall. "I once was lost, but now am found,/Was blind, but now I see." Why? "Amazing grace! how sweet the sound." That's it. God love you.